Your Money Matters: The Finance Fixer's ----- 21 Day Guide ----- on How to Become a Master of Your Money & Win With It!

Your Money Matters: The Finance Fixer's ----- 21 Day Guide ----- on How to Become a Master of Your Money & Win With It!

By Shelbi Threet-White

An Imprint of W.E. Publishing Company, LLC

W.E. Publishing Company, LLC
P.O. Box 1742
Owings Mills, MD 21117
Email: info@wepublishingcompany.com

DEDICATION

This book is dedicated to all that encouraged me, poured into me, believed in me, and cheered for me! I am grateful for you and appreciate you!

FOREWORD

"We Don't Stop for Nobody, Can You Dig It? WOOO, Are You With It? WOOO!!" These were the words from your Author, The Finance Fixer, and Successful Entrepreneurial Guru, Mrs. Shelbi-Threet White and me, Elder Mushir Kinsel, Creative Arts Specialist, Transformative Success Coach and Founder of The Power In You Unlimited. We were just two beautiful little black girls from Junilla Street, in the Hill District of Pittsburgh, Pennsylvania. We spent our days chanting, skipping, arms crossed over each other's shoulders, hearts filled with laughter while singing, "We Don't Stop for Nobody, Can You Dig It? WOOO, Are You With It? WOOO!!" Back then we didn't know or understand that words had power. Who would have known that words, mere child's play, would have become our lifelong silent mantra that manifested, pushed, and propelled our prayers, goals, and dreams into reality?

I have had the pleasure and opportunity of knowing Shelbi my entire life. We literally grew up side by side as neighbors. When it comes down to it, where we come from, real recognizes real. So you can't truly know, address or resolve a problem if you have not felt or experienced the fullness of it. I have witnessed the tumultuous journey of faith, fearless drive and tenacity that shaped and formed this courageous, powerful author.

Your Money Matters, The Finance Fixer's 21 Day Guide to Financial Freedom, is the truth. This guide and resource is power packed. Not only does it provide detailed instructions on how to save money and spend money, but Shelbi also shares the secrets on how to change your habits and thinking regarding money. She shares with you how to recognize the cultural and generational curses connected to your personal relationship and understanding of money and how to break it. Shelbi leads with love and a true desire to see people win. She shares candid, real-life stories and experiences that allows the reader to identify why we spend the way we spend and how to stop the pattern.

Shelbi Threet-White has mastered the art of finding joy in our finances. This book is a game changer. For the reader who is ready to step up to the plate and do the real work…get ready to live out all your dreams, within your means! As Shelbi teaches financial literacy and freedom with a swag and truth, you will be inspired to stay the course and see for yourself the reward she lives in and is now sharing with the world.

We both now reside in the Peach State of Georgia, making the transition from Pennsylvania. Two little black girls from Junilla Street, never stopping, always believing, and living the dream. In all of my conversations around finances with Shelbi, I am consistently left with the infamous line from the classic movie *Baby Boy*, "Are you a Buyer or a Seller," or Shelbi's famous words, "Assets over liabilities"? In her book, she inspires, and initiates thought provoking conversations. By sharing her wisdom, instructions, and personal examples, she provides answers to how you can win in your finances and in your life.

Throughout her journey and rise to financial success and freedom, Shelbi and her husband, David Mark have been a beckon of light by sharing her insights, knowledge, and love with those ready to do the work. If you are reading this, hold on and get ready for the ride of your life!! I wish you peace, power, and love. But remember…DON'T STOP FOR NOBODY!! Can you dig it?

Walk In Power,
Elder Mushir Kinsel

ACKNOWLEDGEMENTS

Father GOD, thank you for choosing me for this project. I have an attitude of gratitude and will forever serve you in JESUS' Name! Amen!

My Husband, thank you for providing for me, protecting me, and pushing me. If I talked about it, you made sure it was brought to fruition. Through the up's downs and all arounds, we always came out victorious! So happy to have you as my life partner and my business partner! I love you endlessly!

Thank you Joycey (Ma) for your commitment in being Reese, Robin, and My Mom. Through you, we learned family, stability, and how life is meant to be lived. To this day, I turn the music up, laugh to it, cry to it, dance to it and celebrate in it! Thank you for your sacrifices! I love you!

My Sisters: Reese & Robin I love you both so much! Glad GOD saw fit for me to be your Lil Sis. I know I was a mess, but what else was a Lil Sis supposed to be? (haha)

To all of my children, bonus children & grandchildren, my prayer is that we will be in one household for Thanksgiving soon and keep it going from there!

Denise & Shavon (Daughters), my Lil Best Friends. The definitions of 'dope daughters'. Thank you both for the continuous love and support!

Robby & Lance (SonSons) It's hard being a Virgo with a Virgo (haha) I'm not perfect, thank you for being patient with me!

Papiiiiiii I love you, and you love me, and we're in LOVE!

Teonna, Aunt Barbara, Mother-In-Law (Roberta), Sis-N-Law (Chas), Patty Wilburn, family and friends who went to be with the LORD, dance forever in paradise! We love you all and miss you so much!

To all my nieces and nephews, Auntieeeeeee LOVES you and supports all of your endeavors! Always strive for GREATNESS!

Aunt Jackie, continue to be strong in life! GOD got you. Press on and be intentional in living your life to the fullest! Aunt Marcy, you are not afraid of life and I love that about you! You are still working hard after retirement. Continue to push through on your new business! I am so happy for you! Aunt Brenda, Uncle Chubb & Uncle Ricky I love you! I have a piece of my Dad in you all here on earth! So thankful!

Twin Cousin Ann, I LOVE you! Thank you for the continuous laughs and uplift! It means everything to me!

My Mother (Joyce Threet), The Cummings (Gil & Robin), The Jones' (Fletch & Shenita), The Smalls (Antoine & Krista), The Bailey's (Rod & Tammy), and Bruce Brown, we are forever grateful to you for loaning us money to get our business started when we were financially unstable, SO VERY GRATEFUL for you all!

To our Best Man & Best Friend, Darwin Copeland, you are simply Z-Best! We are grateful for the talks, the inspiration and the unconditional love! Forever growing!

Lateshya Ellis, you told me I would have 'A Year of Jubilee', I received it and am living in it! An attitude of gratitude for sure!

W.E. Publishing Company, LLC: Thank you for your professionalism, experience and expertise! It was an honor to work with you!

Ineeze Gainey aka 'The Childcare Boss', I'm so glad I invested $97 into your 28 Day Manifestation Class. During the class I told you I was manifesting 'The Finance Fixer', along with my goals. You encouraged me to create an ebook. I took your advice and wrote a whole book (smiling). Shout out to you for this project and Instagram for the connection! Your energy & your vibe is everything! I appreciate you!

Family & Friends, thank you all so much, I am whole heartedly humbled!

TABLE OF CONTENTS

INTRODUCTION

Welcome to: **The Finance Fixer's 21 Day Guide on How to Become A Master of Your Money & Win With It!**

This book was written with 'you' in mind:

'You', who wish to obtain and sustain healthy finance habits; 'You' who just got paid on Friday, and are wondering where your money went by Monday; 'You' who are having a difficult time with creating a budget, or following through with a budget; 'You' who are drowning in debt and don't know the next move to get back on your feet.

You see, I was that 'you' who'd been through all of these financial ups, downs and all arounds. In dealing with financial hardships, I did not have the tools or the resources available to assist me along the way. I tried to do what I thought would work, but those things didn't pan out. After researching how to win with money, I put strategies in place that worked wonders for my finances. I am here to share the tools and the tea on how to live debt free & abundantly.

The time is now to win with those finances and be good stewards of your money. If you start and don't do so well the first time around, it's okay. Rome was not built in one day. Begin again, and as many times as you need to try. Life is about learning and growing through the process. Think of it as a safe/grace zone. It is safe because no judgement is permitted, only grace. Allow yourself God's grace in all things including your finances. Pick up the pieces and continue to move forward in it.

2 Corinthians 9:8

GOD is able to make all things possible. GOD will grant you sufficiency in all things, and even an abundance for every good work.

Studies show it takes 21 days to form a habit. For 21 days, you will be forming the habit of being a good steward of your finances, so that you can make your budget work and win with your money.

CHAPTER 1

Hey it's me, Shelbi

Please allow me to introduce myself:

My name is Shelbi Threet-White.

I am a Pittsburgh native, now residing in the 'Peach State' of Georgia.

I started a business called 'The Finance Fixer' to assist people with their financial goals including: creating a budget that works, cleaning up debt, paying down debt, and of course getting out of debt! I also share tools on how to create a "debt snowball", how to find extra funds within your resources, and finally how to live a stress free life by having your finances in order. The feeling of debt freedom is like no other. I would love everyone reading this book to experience it!

I am passionate about healthy finances because my family and I went through a tumultuous time in our lives when our finances were totally out of order. Our finances were not healthy, to say the least.

CHAPTER 2

How I got here

In 2008, my husband (Dave) was employed for a company in Durham, North Carolina. It was a great job, but the economy had gotten really bad and being that Dave was the last man hired, he was the first man to be let go only 9 months into the job. He applied for other jobs in North Carolina, but to no avail.

Being jobs were scarce in the State of North Carolina; I started applying to jobs in our hometown of Pittsburgh, PA. I had a few calls from Pittsburgh, PA but wasn't ready to move back. After not being able to land a decent job in North Carolina, I had a conversation with my husband. I told him that I was going to take the next job that called from Pittsburgh offering great benefits. And it happened. The University of Pittsburgh called me. I had a telephone interview that went well. The recruiter asked me to come for an in-person interview. I flew back to Pittsburgh and was offered the job. I did not say yes right away because I was not ready to relocate. When I returned to North Carolina, Dave and I spoke about it, and decided it was a good idea. I moved to Pittsburgh first to set everything up for my family. We had only been in North Carolina for one year. The expenses to move to North Carolina and then back to Pittsburgh were very expensive and we took a hit to our savings account.

I worked for the University of Pittsburgh until December of 2009. I left there to accept a better position at the Community College of West Hills. It was a new year and the perfect transition. The college was 5-7 minutes from where we lived, the pay rate was great, and it opened the door for my husband and I to return to school on a tuition reimbursement program.

Dave returned to school on a full time basis for Heating Ventilation and Air Conditioning (HVAC), a skill he wanted to obtain for the goal he was moving towards, which was real estate. He wanted to not only own properties but flip houses. The knowledge he would obtain from the HVAC course would eliminate the need for a 3rd party to do the work on his properties because he would have the skillset to do the work himself.

As a partnership, we agreed that he would return to school while I held the fort down in the household, paying and maintaining the household bills.

Dave was let go from his job in 2009, but he was able to receive unemployment compensation. That helped, because it was additional income in the household.

After six months of being employed with the Community College, I, along with co-workers from my department, were called into the office for an impromptu meeting. During that meeting, we were told that the whole department was being laid off because of 'lack of grant funds'. Although it came as a surprise, it was a bittersweet moment for me. It was bitter because we would have to foot the bill for the remaining semesters of the HVAC program Dave had started, and it was sweet because I was in the process of starting a home daycare, and I no longer had to worry about hiring someone to work. I would be able to work at the daycare on my own. I had been trying to figure out how to operate my daycare for months. I thank GOD he made a way. I was beyond grateful.

CHAPTER 3

A Hot Mess

All things did not fall into place after I was let go from the Community College, however. Dave's compensation had soon exhausted. He started working odd jobs, but nothing on a full time basis because of the rigorous HVAC program. I applied for assistance with unemployment compensation until I got the home daycare up and running, and the process took two months to take effect.

We had an income problem for sure, and bills were starting to pile up. Credit cards began paying our bills. I had a car note which eventually got behind, our rent was behind, and I began to feel like I was drowning--drowning with bills, drowning in my career, and drowning in life.

My daughter Shavon, who was a college student at the time, loved to order food from local restaurants on 'no cafeteria food Friday'. She would call me like clockwork on most Fridays to order her wings and fries, or Philly cheesesteak hoagies & fries, and any other kinds of good food outside of cafeteria food that she ate on a regular basis. She and I would '3 way' call a local restaurant, she would give them her order and I would give them my debit card to place her food order. Soon I was using a credit card. It got to a point where the credit cards were maxed out and I stopped answering her Friday night telephone calls. I was too proud and too embarrassed to tell Shavon I did not have the money to treat her to her wings and fries, or steak hoagie and fries that she anticipated on 'no cafeteria food Friday'.

My son Rob was playing high school sports at this time and all of the sports he participated in had booster fees. I intentionally made sure I did not see the parent that was collecting the fees because I did not have money to give. I had to eventually borrow the fees for him so that he could continue to participate.

One time, our youngest son Lance was invited to a birthday party for a close friend. I went to The Children's Place and put a gift card on my credit card for the birthday boy. When Lance and I arrived at the party place, certain activities required the children to remove their shoes. Lance wanted to do those activities, so he had to remove his sneakers. Once he removed his sneakers, I took them and put them under the table so no one could see them. His sneakers were in horrible shape. That party was in July. When school started in late August, Lance started with that same pair of sneakers. Both my sons (Rob & Lance) started school with raggedy sneakers, but they had clean and decent clothes.

These experiences were humbling.

Talking about stress at a high level! I was stressed to the max trying to figure it all out, which was a huge mistake. I was trying to figure it out by myself as a married woman.

I had always handled the finances, and during the time of this financial crisis, I neglected to have a conversation with my husband. You see, I was once a single mother who had to figure things out on her own. I made things happen on my own, and survived life on my own. I was now a married woman going through one of the hardest trials our marriage had encountered, and yet, I was going through it like I was a single Mom on her own. I went into survival mode and caught myself handling everything all alone.

Once I realized I could no longer do this by myself, I had a conversation with Dave about the 'hot mess'! At this point we were 3 months behind on rent. He was astonished because I never told him about it. I told him about the credit card debt that I had run up. How did he not know? Because he didn't have credit cards; they were all in my name. I told him about my car note being behind. How did he not know? Because it was my car; I had always made the payments.

Rather than blame me, Dave was disappointed that I had taken on this heavy burden on my own. The damage was done. We now had to figure out how we would undo it.

I told Dave I had already started doing research on filing bankruptcy and wanted to proceed with it. That was the only resource I thought was feasible at the time, I just wanted the nightmare of being in a dark and broken financial place to end! I was going to file bankruptcy because everything was in my name and I wanted to make my name good again.

I reached out to an attorney about it. A few weeks later, I met with the attorney so I could pursue filing the bankruptcy. The attorney's fee was $1500. And I thought to myself: Here we go again. Where am I going to get $1500 from!

A bankruptcy hearing was scheduled, and I didn't show up for it. I didn't show up because I was too embarrassed to tell the attorney I didn't have $1500. Communication was definitely an issue I had. I never wanted to face hardships. I used to try and pray them away. That *did not* work. I had to start facing my fears head on.

9

Eventually I came up with the fee of $1500 and took it to the attorney's office. He scheduled another hearing. The $1500 attorney fee was borrowed from a family member and it was a struggle to repay the family member back. I had gotten in a serious rut!

CHAPTER 4

The assignment

After the bankruptcy, I did not have the proper tools to start over. My finances were still out of order. Dave and I were still struggling. We opened the home daycare, which was located in our first rental property. This started to be a concern because I included this property in the bankruptcy. It was only a matter of time before I would have to vacate the premises.

One day Dave and I were riding through the Troy Hill section of the Northside. We passed by a shopping plaza where my daughter Shavon went to preschool when she was three years old. As we drove past, we noticed a 'for rent' sign in the window. I mentioned to Dave it would be a nice space to start a daycare center.

On the way home, I asked Dave if he could ride back through the area and get the telephone number from the sign posted in the window, and he did.

The following day, I made contact with the building manager. She let me know that the space was last a Doctor's office and had been vacant for 4 years. My thought was that it was 'a diamond in the rough' because there were no childcare facilities in the area. There was one problem, though. Dave & I didn't have adequate finances to rent the building.

During this time, I was listening to a disc that my Cousin, Tracie had given me over a year prior. Dave and I were driving one day and he put the disc in the car's CD player. The disc was from a Women's Conference my Cousin Tracie had attended in Houston Texas. The CD had sat in the car for over a year without getting my attention. The name of the woman on the CD was Stacia Pierce.

Stacia's message was "When you pray, do not just sit on it, have big faith and move toward whatever it is you're praying for."

I thought about the building in Troy Hill for a few days. I also thought about how I could get this building with no money! Stacia Pierce's voice urged me to MOVE! I did just that! I called and scheduled a meeting to see the space with Eleanor, the Building Manager.

Upon meeting Eleanor, I saw the space, and realized it was in horrible condition. It smelled bad. There was an infestation of stink bugs, and it would be quite a big job to clean the place up! I told my husband about it and we scheduled another time to see the space. My husband is a visionary. As we were walking through the space, he started imagining how to set the place up, and I started to get excited. We told Eleanor we were interested, and she gave us an application to complete. There was a space on the application that asked for bank account information and two personal references (Thank you Poopsie and Krista). I was good for the personal references, but our bank account was not so good. At that time, our balance was negative $67.

Eleanor phoned us a week later and scheduled a time to meet at the Lowrie Street space. We met her, and she did not mention a negative report. I don't know if she checked our bank account, but she had great news! We were approved for the building and she had a lease and keys in hand! I could hardly believe we got the building!

We asked Eleanor if she could extend 3 months of non-payment towards the rent so that we could transform a doctor's office to a childcare center. Not only did we need to transform the space, but we did not have the funds to pay the rent. We started REALLY borrowing money from family and friends. This facility had to work! It was our only way out of the rut we were in. I began scheduling meetings with a few friends and family members. I drew up a plan for each of them and told them what was needed to get this child care facility up and running.

Each friend and each relative who I presented with my pitch gave what they could, and to each one of them we are grateful! It was a struggle to get each person paid back while we were short on funds, but we did it.

Then it started again. I began using credit cards to pay for everything and was being careless with our finances. I saw myself putting my family in the same predicament and going down the same rabbit hole.

CHAPTER 5

Assignment understood

A decision needed to be made that I would respect. I had to shift my mindset in the way I was thinking about money, and how I was treating money which was careless. I had to get a grip. If I wanted to be in charge of my household's money, I needed to put my whole life in order, starting with my mindset, and I did. I'm grateful to my husband for trusting me, not judging me, and never-not once- throwing the fact that 'I screwed up' in my face!

So I got to work! I started researching everything that had to do with financial literacy.

I studied, was disciplined, and though I messed up a few more times, did not stop. I kept going. My husband and I were of one accord and realized we had to sow different, think different, and move different, in order to reap different.

When invited out to events, we had to decline a lot of things because we did not have the funds to attend them. If we did attend an event, it was all inclusive and we did not go to the mall to shop for new clothes. We shopped in our own closets.

During this time, we had to endure so much to build! Our childcare center went through two contractors, two electricians, and two plumbers! Most of them took advantage of us. This led to Dave being his own general contractor.

Our bankruptcy led me to give birth to 'The Finance Fixer'. I developed systems that helped me to be a good steward of our finances, as well as assist others with theirs.

Our car repossession was so embarrassing! This led us to pay our car notes until they got down to $0. The foreclosure on our first rental property that we had refinanced led us to avoid refinancing in the future. Dave started doing sheriff sales and paying cash for investment properties. I got laid off from my job while Dave was in an extensive HVAC program. This led us to develop multiple streams of income so if one was laid off, the other income could cover the loss.

Our children that were in college could not call us for anything. Not even takeout. We did not have it to give. It was a lesson on living, learning and saving. I felt extremely bad that I could not provide for our children at the time, but they learned perseverance during their college years. Our oldest daughter Denise (Quay) had a side hustle doing eyelashes out of her college apartment and Shavon ran a candy store out of her dorm room.

We had to borrow money from family & friends to start different businesses.

I'm so grateful to them! They gave us what we needed for a great start! I didn't want to get out of bed some days! And YES I wanted to give up every time we were tested in this endeavor.

But GOD! We continued to trust HIM!

Our lifestyle shifted. A lot was different. Dave & I even dated differently, but we did not stop dating. Instead of going out and spending money in restaurants, and using up gas driving to those restaurants, we dated at our home with dinner, a movie, candles, and with our favorite songs playing. We got to choose our favorite songs and danced together. Till this day, we eat great meals, put on great music and dance the night away in the comfort of our own home.

We even do TikToks together. It has definitely brought us closer together than ever, and for that we are grateful to GOD.

We did everything necessary to keep ourselves from going backwards. By starting, never stopping, making wise choices and a few big changes in our lives, my family and I started to see an upswing and wins in our finances. We continued to press forward with the process that was working for us: budgeting, not eating out, shopping our closets and having to say no to events that were not within our budget. With a few shifts and a lot of shuffles, we were starting to see the light. Assignment understood!

My husband and I are now winning with our finances, so much so, we relocated to another state and paid cash for the move. How? We made a plan and stuck to the plan, we made a budget and stuck to the budget, we trusted the process and we rolled out (smiling).

I want you to win too. It's such a GREAT feeling!

Fixing your finances is a mindset. I highly suggest you fix your finances before you fix your credit.

The reason for this being:

If you fix your credit without first shifting your mindset to maintain healthy finance habits, you will end up with bad credit again, and the cycle will continue to repeat itself. Those credit cards will be used and abused again because you were not given the tools on how to keep your credit good. Credit repair companies will fix your credit but still leave you with poor finance habits. You cannot win without the correct resources and/or you don't change your mindset.

CHAPTER 6

Let's work!

Within this book, you will be given the tools on how to obtain, maintain and sustain healthy finance habits.

Now let's get to the great feeling of winning with your money!

For 21 days, we will be discussing ways to maintain and sustain healthy finance habits.

Each day, you will be given a task. Please make a commitment to stay on task for 21 days so that these tasks can become habits. At the end of the 21 days a habit will be formed, and you will start getting ahead with your finances!

Job 22:28 states:

"You shall decree a thing and it will be established for you, and the light of GOD's favor will shine upon your ways."

At the top of each page, I need you to decree a thing so it will be established for you.

We are decreeing and declaring:

It's winning season! I will win with my money! I will be a good steward of my money!

These tasks will take time, patience and commitment. Put at least 20-30 minutes to the side each day to complete each task. Get a pen and take notes on the pages provided within this book.

Decree & Declare Greatness
Journal Entry

_____

_____

_____

_____

_____

_____

_____

_____

_____

_____

_____

_____

_____

_____

_____

_____

_____

_____

_____

_____

_____

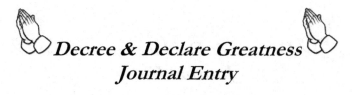

Decree & Declare Greatness
Journal Entry

_____

_____

_____

_____

_____

_____

_____

_____

_____

_____

_____

_____

_____

_____

_____

_____

_____

_____

_____

_____

_____

CHAPTER 7

Let's define the word Budget

Why is the word 'budget' so taboo?

A budget is telling your money where to go, instead of wondering where it went. With a budget, you control your money and do not let your money control you. With a budget, you will give every one of your dollars a name.

Example:	
Shoes:	$100
Coat:	$125
Rug:	$250
Total	**$475**

This is an example of giving every dollar a name. Make a plan with your money, so you can always win with money! Keep in mind, you are the ruler of your money, do not allow money to rule you!

CHAPTER 8

Your Turn

Task 1

ON THE BLANK PAGES WRITE:

I decree & declare:

It's WINNING SEASON! I will WIN with my money! I will be a good steward of my money!

Now that you have decreed & declared success, LET'S WIN!

What are 3 things you would like to change about the way you handle your finances?

Write them on the pages provided.

'NO JUDGE ZONE'! Give yourself grace. We are all in this together, and we will WIN TOGETHER!

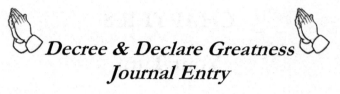

Decree & Declare Greatness
Journal Entry

_____

_____

_____

_____

_____

_____

_____

_____

_____

_____

_____

_____

_____

_____

_____

_____

_____

_____

_____

_____

List 3 things you would like to change about the way you handle your finances $$:

1. _____

   _____

   _____

   _____

   _____

2. _____

   _____

   _____

   _____

3. _____

   _____

   _____

   _____

   _____

Task 1A

Visualization:

VISUALIZATION *TASK 1A*

Pull up your bank statements for the last three months. Study your bank statement for approximately 15-20 minutes. What do you spend your money on the most? Would you like to spend less in that category? Think of ways you can spend less in that category.

Task 1A
Journal Entry

_____

_____

_____

_____

_____

_____

_____

_____

_____

_____

_____

_____

_____

_____

_____

_____

Task 1A
Journal Entry

_____

_____

_____

_____

_____

_____

_____

_____

_____

_____

_____

_____

_____

_____

_____

_____

_____

_____

_____

Task 2

Download the 'Every Dollar' budgeting app., and create an account for it:
www.ramseysolutions.com/ramseyplus/everydollar

This can be done on a desktop, laptop or your cell phone.

This is the app we will use going forward to start budgeting. After you download the app, take a look at it and its categories. Remove categories that do not apply to you and feel free to add categories that you will use when budgeting.

Being that you picked this book up and have made it this far, I trust that you are making a conscious decision to change the way you are thinking about your finances. On a daily basis, schedule a time that you will commit to work on your finances. Do not get distracted by social media, telephone calls or anything else. Create a quiet serene space, and let's get to working hard on winning with your finances!

Task 3

Let's decree & declare and write at the top page of the pages provided....

It's winning season! I will win with my money, I will be a good steward of my money! Now let's win!

Income

How much income is coming into your household on a monthly basis? Income includes paychecks, unemployment compensation, child support, side hustle, extra job, etc.

Add all of your income information to the 'Every Dollar' budgeting app., under 'INCOME'.

Please note:

Creating a budget is a process. Slow and steady will win the race!

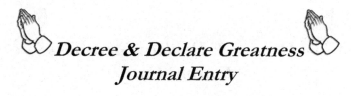

Decree & Declare Greatness
Journal Entry

_____

_____

_____

_____

_____

_____

_____

_____

_____

_____

_____

_____

_____

_____

_____

_____

_____

_____

_____

Decree & Declare Greatness
Journal Entry

_____

_____

_____

_____

_____

_____

_____

_____

_____

_____

_____

_____

_____

_____

_____

_____

_____

_____

_____

Task 4

LET'S DECREE & DECLARE!

It's winning season! I will win with my money, I will be a good steward of my money! Say it loud, and write it on the pages provided.

Let's chit chat about the word 'budget'.

A budget does not restrict you from spending money or living the life that you want to live. With a budget your money is being tracked. A budget actually gives you the freedom to spend, but within that spending you will know where every one of your dollars are going.

Do not let the song fool you "we work too hard to be balling on a budget"! ["My Last" by Big Sean / Chris Brown] Absolutely NOT. We work too hard to NOT be balling on a budget. Why would you work hard, NOT budget your money, ball out and overdraft your account? Let's make some sense here. Work hard, budget your money, ball out and win! It's genius! I promise, you will win every time! It's order and alignment.

Now let's get into it!!

Gather all of your household bills.

Household bills include:

Mortgage / Rent, light, gas, water, sewage, cable, internet, groceries, eating out / sports and entertainment, Netflix, Hulu, cell phone, home phone, etc.

Task 5

Let's decree & declare! It's winning season! I will win with my money! I will be a good steward of my money!

Remember to write this at the top of your page on a daily basis.

Budget continued:

As you gather your bills, begin to enter them into the categories on the 'Every Dollar' budgeting app., or on the pages provided.

Enter the bill name example (such as Verizon) as well as the bill amount. It's okay if you paid $100 on your cell phone bill last month but it's $130 this month. Every Dollar is flexible. Your budget will allow you to change the amounts and categories on an 'as needed' basis.

When budgeting your money, you are giving every one of your dollars a name, i.e. Mortgage-$1,000; Light- $150.00; Gas- $200.

Also, this is when that 'scheduled time for finances' is needed. Put in the work so you can win. Take your time during this task. Be patient and diligent.

Decree & Declare Greatness
Journal Entry

_____

_____

_____

_____

_____

_____

_____

_____

_____

_____

_____

_____

_____

_____

_____

_____

_____

_____

_____

Decree & Declare Greatness
Journal Entry

_____

_____

_____

_____

_____

_____

_____

_____

_____

_____

_____

_____

_____

_____

_____

_____

_____

_____

_____

Task 6

BUDGET CONTINUED:

Now let's take a look at those other categories you spend money on:

Car insurance, clothes, subscriptions, Amazon and other websites, etc.

Enter these categories in the 'Every Dollar' budgeting app., or on the pages provided.

Keep in mind this is a part of budgeting: you are telling your money where to go instead of wondering where it went.

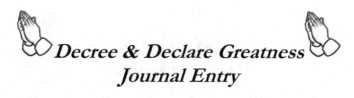

Decree & Declare Greatness
Journal Entry

_____

_____

_____

_____

_____

_____

_____

_____

_____

_____

_____

_____

_____

_____

_____

_____

_____

_____

_____

Decree & Declare Greatness
Journal Entry

_____

_____

_____

_____

_____

_____

_____

_____

_____

_____

_____

_____

_____

_____

_____

_____

_____

_____

_____

_____

_____

_____

_____

Task 7

OVERVIEW AND CHECK IN:

Let's chit chat.

How is everything going?

Did you enter all of your bills in the 'Every Dollar' budgeting app., or on the pages provided?

If you left something out, it's okay, you can always go back and add the categories you think of and switch things out as needed.

It takes approximately 3 months to perfect a budget. Do NOT get discouraged, stay steadfast and on task.

Task 8

SAY IT LOUD!

It's WINNING SEASON! I will WIN with my money! I will be a good steward of my money! Now let's win!

What extra money are you giving away every month? Do you have subscriptions to things that you don't use? Do you have Cable, Netflix, Prime TV & HULU? Do you watch all of this? Consider getting rid of one or two of these things to free up some of your hard earned cash.

Are you paying a subscription to have a massage every month, but go every 3 months? Get rid of subscriptions and pay as you go.

Are you paying to get a car wash 'anytime' but only go every few months? Get rid of that subscription, and pay when you go.

These companies prey on people knowing they won't utilize it as often as they should. GET RID OF IT and free up some of that hard earned money that you work for.

What about eating out? I'm not saying 'do not' eat out....I'm saying BUDGET for eating out and be REAL about it. Once that 'eat out' budget is exhausted, start preparing meals at home. Yes, it is time consuming, but once you see how much money you are spending on 'eating out' you will be encouraged to ease up on it.

Task 9

DEBT:

We will be discussing the infamous and dreadful word 'debt' including credit cards, student loans, car loans, etc.

First up:

Let's chit chat about credit cards. How many do you have? Are they current? If they are not current, are they with a collection agency?

Why do you use credit cards instead of debit cards or cash?

Are you responsible when you use your credit cards, keeping the utilization low?

Decree & Declare Greatness
Journal Entry

_____

_____

_____

_____

_____

_____

_____

_____

_____

_____

_____

_____

_____

_____

_____

_____

_____

_____

_____

_____

_____

Decree & Declare Greatness
Journal Entry

_____

_____

_____

_____

_____

_____

_____

_____

_____

_____

_____

_____

_____

_____

_____

_____

_____

Task 10

DEBT CONTINUED:

Gather all of your monthly debt including credit cards, car note, student loans, doctors' bills, etc. Once you gather your debt, put them in the 'Debt Category' of the 'Every Dollar' budgeting app., or the pages provided along with the monthly payments.

CONGRATS! You created a budget!

December 2021 ⌄

| Planned | Spent | Remaining |

$4,000
monthly income

$219.88 left to budget

INCOME	PLANNED
Paycheck 1	$2,000.00
Paycheck 2	$1,500.00
Side Hustle	$500.00
Add Income	

December 2021 ⌄

| Planned | Spent | Remaining |

$219.88 left to budget

HOUSING	PLANNED
Mortgage/Rent	$1,450.00
Light Bill	$200.00
Water/Sewage	$100.00
Trash	$66.00
Add Item	

TRANSPORTATION	PLANNED
Auto Gas & Oil	$100.00
Car Replacement	$10.00
Add Item	

December 2021 ⌄

| Planned | Spent | Remaining |

$219.88 left to budget

INSURANCE & TAX	PLANNED
Life Insurance	$29.47
College Fund	$50.00
Retirement	$100.00
Life Insurance	$127.68
Dental Insurance	$64.00
Health Insurance	$123.00
Add Item	

December 2021 ⌄

| Planned | Spent | Remaining |

$219.88 left to budget

LIFESTYLE	PLANNED
Me Monthly	$100.00
Husband Monthly	$100.00
Son Monthly	$50.00
Netflix	$14.97
Internet	$45.00
Add Item	

Task 11

DEBT SNOWBALLING:

Let's chit chat about debt snowballing

Let's define what a Debt Snowball is.

A debt snowball is a debt reduction strategy in which you pay off bills in order of the smallest to the largest regardless of the interest rate. But it's more than a method of paying off bills. The debt snowball is designed to help you change how you behave with money so you never go into debt again. It forces you to stay intentional about paying one bill at a time until you are debt-free, and it gives you power over your debt.

When you pay off that first bill and move on to the next, you'll see that debt is not the boss of your money, you are! I LOVE debt snowballing!

With the debt snowball method, Dave and I paid off four credit cards, his student loan (which he had for over 20 years), and two car loans.

Task 12

DEBT SNOWBALLING CONTINUED:

Now that your budget is made, and you've entered your debt info in the 'Every Dollar App' as advised in Task 10, on the blank pages provided, write 'Debt Snowballing' at the top of the page.

Step 1:

From your Every Dollar App, write your debt from the lowest balance and the amount owed, to the highest balance and the amount owed. Also, list the due dates of each debt. Be sure to include all of your debt;

Credit Cards

Car loans

Student loans

Doctors Bills

Etc.

(Minus your mortgage/rent)

Debt Snowball
Worksheet

Payment Priority	Debt Name	Interest Rate (%)	Minimum Monthly Payment

Task 13

DEBT SNOWBALLING CONTINUED:

Step 2:

Make minimum payments on all of your debts except the smallest debt.

Step 3:

Pay as much as possible on your smallest debt.

When you were asked to eliminate subscriptions, and other things that you are paying for on a monthly basis, and aren't using, this is the extra money that can be used towards paying on the smallest debt of the debt snowball.

Step 4:

Repeat until each debt is paid in full.

This will become a cycle.

Once that 1st debt is paid off, you will take funds from the 1st paid off debt and apply those monies to the 2nd debt on your debt snowball.

This process will have a snowball effect. The momentum will pick up and paying off debt will become exciting!

Well it did for me!

Example of a Debt Snowball

List your smallest debt to largest debt

Example				
Payment Priority	**Debt Name**	**Interest Rate**	**Debt Amount**	**Minimum Monthly Amount**
1	Credit Card A (Discover Card)	21.4%	$500	Balance due $20.00
2	Credit Card B (Chase Card)	20.5%	$600	Balance due $50.00
3	Credit Card C (American Ex)	18%	$1,000	Balance due $75.00
4	Doctors Bill	N/A	$2,000	Balance due $100.00
5	Student Loan	15%	$10,000	Balance due $150.00
6	Car Payment	10%	$20,000	Balance due $300.00
	Total		**$34,100**	**Balance due $695.00**

54

The goal is to eliminate this debt. We will start with the smallest debt, which is the Discover Card. You will take as much as you can out of the 'extra funds' you created and start paying more than $20.00 on the Discover Card. For example, you got rid of Hulu so that is an extra $60.00 added to your income. Discover Card will receive $80.00. You will continue to pay the minimum balances on the other cards until the Discover Card is paid in full.

Once the Discover Card is paid in full, you will cut that card up and use it no more.

You will then move to the next card which is Chase. You were paying $50.00 on Chase, but now that the Discover Card is paid off, you have an extra $80 to apply to Chase. You are now paying $130.00 towards your Chase card. Once your Chase card is paid off, you will cut it up and not use it again. The goal is to eliminate debt.

Let's move to your 3rd Credit Card which is American Express. You have a $1,000 balance due and your monthly payment is $75.00. You paid off your Discover Card and your Chase Card and have $130.00 additional to pay towards that $1,000 balance on your American Express Card. This is why it is called a 'Debt Snowball'. As you continue to move on, your payments towards the next debt becomes bigger. It's a great system and it works!! Remember, only grace is given. If you mess up, it's okay, pick up the pieces and start again. It takes approximately three months to perfect a budget. Make changes and adjustments as needed.

Task 14

CREDIT CARDS:

If you are getting credit card offers in the mail, I advise you to look at them.

A lot of times their 'low interest' introductory offers can save you money.

Call the company who sent the offer and inquire about transferring your 'high balance' credit cards to the 'low interest' introductory offer. If they allow you to transfer the balance, CONGRATS!

Now here is where it gets tough. You now have a credit card with a $0 balance because of the transfer you just made. I need you to cut that credit card up and leave it at a $0 balance. Please do not run the balance up. It will defeat the purpose of getting out of debt. Remember, we are practicing healthy finance habits.

The goal is to pay down debt.

Task 15

CAR NOTE/CAR PAYMENTS:

Let's chit chat about car payments.

Do you have a car payment? What is your end goal with your car? Do you want another one; are you going to keep this one? Is it financed or leased?

If you have an interest rate of more than 7%, I highly recommend you try to refinance your vehicle. If you refinance your vehicle, you can save on your monthly payment and also eliminate months off of your balance due.

Tip: Do not go out and purchase another car while you still have a car payment on your current car.

The car dealer will tack the balance of what you owe on your current car to the new car. This is called a 'ROLL OVER'!!!!

The dealer will be quick to tell you it won't be much....but are they paying the 'it won't be much'?!?! NO THEY ARE NOT......YOU ARE! DO NOT DO IT!!!! It's predatory and they are not going to be responsible for the debt. You are!

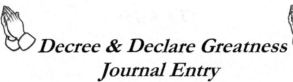

Decree & Declare Greatness
Journal Entry

_____

_____

_____

_____

_____

_____

_____

_____

_____

_____

_____

_____

_____

_____

_____

_____

_____

_____

_____

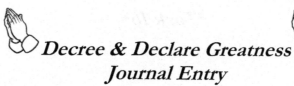

Decree & Declare Greatness
Journal Entry

_____

_____

_____

_____

_____

_____

_____

_____

_____

_____

_____

_____

_____

_____

_____

_____

_____

_____

Task 16

SINKING FUNDS:

Let's chit chat about 'sinking funds'.

A sinking fund is a fund containing money to save for a major purchase, or a purchase that does not meet the monthly budget.

The sinking fund helps to soften the hardship.

Examples of a sinking fund:

1. You have a $1,000 tax debt due every year in March. You will put $83 of your money each month into your 'sinking fund' from March of this year to March of next year.

When a year rolls around, 'VOILA' the $1,000 is in your fund and you don't have to be stressed about where this extra $1,000 is coming from.

2. You know you want to go on a dream vacation in 2 years. You also know that dream vacation will cost approximately $2,000. You will put $200 per month in a savings account that you do not have a debit card to, so when it's time to plan the trip, your $2,000 will be saved, your trip will be paid for, and you will have money to buy extra clothes for the dream vacation.

3. I also would recommend a Christmas Club account that can be set up through a bank or Credit Union.

How a Christmas Club account works.

You would go to your local bank or Credit Union and tell them you would like to open a Christmas Club account. Once your Christmas Club account is opened, you will contact your payroll department, and advise them you opened a Christmas Club account, give them your Christmas Club account information and tell them how much you would like to be deducted from your paycheck. The funds deducted, will be deposited into your Christmas Club account. When the Holiday season comes around, the funds from the Christmas Club account will be given to you. Some banks or credit unions will send you a check, if you already have an account with the establishment, they will sometimes direct deposit it into your checking account. Speak to your banker to get information on how their establishment disburses Christmas Club funds.

#SinkingFunds

#ConsiderIt

#AvoidsCreditCardDebt

#NoStress

#DebtFreedom

$$ List <u>SINKING FUNDS</u> that will work for you $$:

1. _____
   _____
   _____
   _____
   _____

2. _____
   _____
   _____
   _____
   _____

3. _____
   _____
   _____
   _____
   _____

$$ List __SINKING FUNDS__ that will work for you $$:

4. _____

_____

_____

_____

_____

5. _____

_____

_____

_____

_____

6. _____

_____

_____

_____

_____

Task 17

This is another 'free up your funds' task so that you can have extra money in your budget to clear up some debt.

Car Insurance:

Are you paying a decent cost for car insurance, or did you go with the first quote that you were given?

It's always good to shop around.

Call these numbers to get quotes and see if they can save you money.

Every dollar helps!

If you can save, apply those extra funds to your debt!
#Discipline
#CallNow

State Farm-1-800-782-8332
Amica- 1-800-242-6244
All State-1-877-366-1607

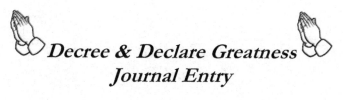

Decree & Declare Greatness
Journal Entry

_____

_____

_____

_____

_____

_____

_____

_____

_____

_____

_____

_____

_____

_____

_____

_____

_____

_____

_____

Decree & Declare Greatness
Journal Entry

_____

_____

_____

_____

_____

_____

_____

_____

_____

_____

_____

_____

_____

_____

_____

_____

_____

_____

_____

_____

_____

Task 18

FINANCE CHECK IN:

Let's take a closer look at your income, the debt you eliminated and tracking your expenses.

Write these questions on the blank page provided and answer them:

Is your income covering all of your expenses?

When you eliminate the unnecessary things, are you seeing more of your money?

Track your expenses in your 'Every Dollar' budgeting app."

If you drive through Chick-Fil-A, before you drive off, pull over into a parking space, pull out your telephone, go on your 'Every Dollar' budgeting app., and put the amount you just spent in your 'Eat out/Restaurant' category.

Make this a habit. It's a very good habit to have. When you make this a common practice, you will see where your money is going instead of wondering where it went.

Decree & Declare Greatness
Journal Entry

_____

_____

_____

_____

_____

_____

_____

_____

_____

_____

_____

_____

_____

_____

_____

_____

_____

_____

Decree & Declare Greatness
Journal Entry

_____

_____

_____

_____

_____

_____

_____

_____

_____

_____

_____

_____

_____

_____

_____

_____

_____

Task 19

EXTRA INCOME:

If you are spending more than you bring in, then consider at least two of these things:

1. Get an extra job such as Lyft, Uber, DoorDash, UberEats etc. I recommend these companies because you can set your own schedule. Set a goal that you want to reach to pay off extra debt, which will lead to debt elimination.

2. Eliminate unnecessary spending. If you are eating out 5 days a week, cut it down to 3 days a week.

Start thinking about meal prepping on a night that fits your schedule. My meal prep day is Sunday. While cooking Sunday dinner, I also prepare meals for the week.

Some of the meals I prep:

Spaghetti for Monday:
Brown ground beef/turkey/chicken (eliminate if you do not eat meat)
Cook spaghetti noodles
Put ground meat in a container and refrigerate (eliminate if you do not eat meat)
Put spaghetti noodles in container and refrigerate
On Monday, add your sauce to your meat of choice or just your noodles, and there you have spaghetti for Monday. This

cuts down meal prep time for working parents in the household.

Taco Tuesday:
Ground meat of your choice that you prepped on Sunday. Take a portion of the meat you browned, and add taco seasoning to it.
Add your toppings to your Taco.
I sauté shrimp on Sundays and have shrimp fajitas on Tuesday. My husband and youngest son still enjoy the ground turkey for Taco Tuesday.
You can also sauté chicken breast for a yummy fajita. Whatever your choice is, pre-prep it for a great meal. These are just suggestions. Do whatever your preference is.

Wednesday pull your sautéed chicken or shrimp out, and all of your salad toppings for a yummy shrimp or chicken salad. If you have left over shrimp, you can make 5 minute grits and there is your Thursday meal. Meal prepping can be simple meals, or you can prep large meals. Again, these are just suggestions so you can save money and not have to worry about what you are cooking the next day. Make it fun and do not make it hard. Open the fridge, heat up your options and continue your day with less prep time for meal time.

*Budget by all means available! Eliminate debt by any means necessary!

List meals you can prepare weekly:

1. _____

_____

_____

_____

_____

2. _____

_____

_____

_____

_____

3. _____

_____

_____

_____

_____

List meals you can prepare weekly:

4. _____

_____

_____

_____

_____

5. _____

_____

_____

_____

_____

6. _____

_____

_____

_____

_____

Task 20

SAVINGS ACCOUNT:

There is nothing like seeing your hard earned money sitting in a high yielding savings account. The more you save, the more you are going to want to save. Saving money gives you the feeling of accomplishment, triumph, joy, and comfort.

If you've had problems saving in the past, I would suggest 'saving without thinking about it'. Open up a savings account with a bank or credit union that is not convenient for you to get to. You can have the bank or credit union automatically withdraw funds from your paycheck and those funds will go directly to your savings account. Do NOT get a debit card for this savings account. The goal is to save.

The finance guru "Dave Ramsey" states you should save $1,000 fast for your starter emergency fund, and after your debt is paid off, he suggests you should save 3-6 months of expenses in a fully funded emergency fund.

This is great advice from Dave Ramsey. If an emergency arises, you won't have to pull out a credit card and go into debt. You will be able to go into your savings account and pay for the emergency with YOUR cash.

Task 21

In order for your finances to be in order, a shift is required.

Clear the clutter. Clutter has a cumulative effect on our brains. Our brains adapt to order. The visual distraction of clutter increases cognitive overload and causes stress. If you want your finances to be in order, a shift is necessary. Clear the clutter. Whether it's negative conversation or organizing your closet, clear the clutter. Go through that junk mail and put it in the trash. Let it go!

Get rid of those old bills. I suggest keeping bills from 2 months prior to make sure your payments were applied correctly. When you see it was applied correctly, get rid of it, TRASH IT!

Clean your space and light a candle. Put your shoes in your closet neatly. Clear the clutter off of your dresser. Everything should have a place.

When everything is in order, you will feel so much better!

Clear the clutter and make room for your newly organized financial life and financial wins!

Clear the clutter and get that budget right & tight!

Continue to decree & declare and take control over your finances!!

Job 22:28 says......

"Thou shalt also decree a thing, and it shall be established unto thee: and the light shall shine upon thy ways."

In closure, I am decreeing & declaring that every person reading this book will follow these tasks.
And in following the tasks, you will create the best budgets ever, eliminate unnecessary debt, pay down debt, sustain financial freedom, start saving and make wise investments.

Create a quiet space, set the mood for positive energy, believe that you can, know that you deserve it, walk through it and come out victorious!

Remember, slow and steady wins the race. Do not give up! There is no success without sacrifice. When you are intentional in being a good steward of your money, you will win with your money and that is the end goal.

If you really want to do something, you'll find a way, if you don't you'll find an excuse. ~Jim Rohn

No excuses here! You will win with your money and be good stewards of your money. You will become debt free and live abundantly. You will work hard and sacrifice. And lastly, you will celebrate your success.

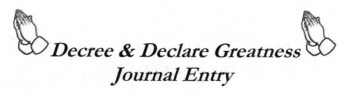

Decree & Declare Greatness
Journal Entry

_____

_____

_____

_____

_____

_____

_____

_____

_____

_____

_____

_____

_____

_____

_____

_____

_____

_____

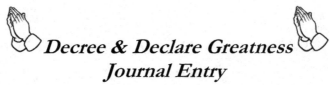

Decree & Declare Greatness
Journal Entry

_____

_____

_____

_____

_____

_____

_____

_____

_____

_____

_____

_____

_____

_____

_____

_____

_____

_____

_____

_____

_____

Decree & Declare Greatness
Journal Entry

Decree & Declare Greatness
Journal Entry

_____

_____

_____

_____

_____

_____

_____

_____

_____

_____

_____

_____

_____

_____

_____

_____

_____

_____

_____

_____

_____

_____

Decree & Declare Greatness
Journal Entry

_____

_____

_____

_____

_____

_____

_____

_____

_____

_____

_____

_____

_____

_____

_____

_____

REFERENCES

1. Ramsey, D. (2022). Every Dollar. Tell your money where to go instead of wondering where it went. Retrieved on February 1, 2022, from http://www.ramseysolutions.com
2. Rohn, J. (1997). Success Presents Jim Rohn International. Retrieved on February 1, 2022, from http://www.jimrohn.com
3. Allstate Insurance, http://allstate.com, 1-877-366-1607
4. Amica, http://www.insurance.amica.com, 1-800-242-6244
5. State Farm, http://www.statefarm.com, 1-800-782-8332

ABOUT THE AUTHOR

Shelbi Threet-White is a Wife, Mother, and a successful Serial Entrepreneur. The self-proclaimed 'Finance Fixer' was born and raised in the Hill District of Pittsburgh, Pennsylvania.

From humble beginnings, she learned the value and reward of hard work, and realized that God was using her to be an example and light in a place where darkness had been accepted as the norm.

Chasing her dream to create a hub for family and community, Shelbi and her husband, Dave embarked on their first business, 'Shelbi's Beauty Supplies Plus', which was an African American Beauty Supply Store located in the West End of Pittsburgh.

As their knowledge of entrepreneurship grew, they laid the foundation for their next business endeavor and opened a community based Childcare Center, 'A Tot's Spot Daycare' which was located in the Troy Hill section of the Northside of Pittsburgh.

The success of their childcare business proved what Shelbi's cousin, Tracey had always told her, "if you build it, they will come". Shelbi used that literally and figuratively as she and her husband launched their real estate company, 'DS White Enterprises, LLC' where they invest in real estate properties to flip, buy, and hold homes for rental investments.

They have expanded their real estate ventures to their new hometown of Georgia.

With every business, and every level of achievement, there were also obstacles. There was a tumultuous time in Shelbi's life where her family's finances were totally out of order and became an issue.

Out of that financial hardship, Shelbi learned many lessons, found her passion, and turned it into blessings.

She began hosting 'free' finance and budget workshops on the weekends at the childcare center. Her goal was to educate the masses on how to win with money and become good financial stewards.

Shelbi was so passionate about helping people win their finances, that she took her passion to the next level. In February 2020, she birthed 'The Finance Fixer'. The 'Finance Fixer' is a coaching program that educates people on how to manage money, budget money, win with money and build wealth with money.

In the pages of this book, you will find financial woes that turned into wins for Shelbi and her family. The 21 day guide to getting your finances right & tight gives instruction on how you can make wise financial wins. It discusses how you can take control of your money, and tell your money where to go instead of wondering where it went.

With the tools provided, you too can become good stewards and be on the winning side of your money! Dig in and let's win!

Made in the USA
Columbia, SC
08 February 2025

53551677R00059